HAL LEONARD SCHOOL FOR
SNARE DRUM
A BEGINNING DRUM METHOD

BY BEN HANS AND JOHN S. PRATT

EDITED BY RICK MATTINGLY

For our teachers, Evan Fisher and Norman Pe

ISBN 978-1-4234-4406-0

HAL•LEONARD®
CORPORATION
7777 W. BLUEMOUND RD. P.O. BOX 13819 MILWAUKEE, WI 53213

In Australia Contact:
Hal Leonard Australia Pty. Ltd.
4 Lentara Court
Cheltenham, Victoria, 3192 Australia
Email: ausadmin@halleonard.com.au

Visit Hal Leonard Online at
www.halleonard.com

TABLE OF CONTENTS

FOREWORD

By Rick Mattingly

There always seems to be an emphasis on the "new" in music: the newest stars, the newest songs, the newest styles. But look just below the surface and you'll find a deep well of tradition. Listen to field recordings of African chants from the early 20th century and you can't help but be reminded of rap. Listen to current pop and hear the influence of the blues. And how about all those hot young guitar players flailing away on their Fender Stratocasters—the same guitar Buddy Holly played in the 1950s.

With drummers, the equipment has changed to encompass electronics for drumset players, while drums corps have replaced rope-tuned, wood-rimmed, calfskin-headed drums with instruments featuring high-tension lugs, steel hoops, and heads made of the same material as bulletproof vests. But the drumming itself hasn't changed all that much. It's still built on whole, half, quarter, eighth, and sixteenth notes, and whether the players know it or not, much of what they play is based on patterns defined as "rudiments" in 1933 by the National Association of Rudimental Drummers.

But times change, and however much today's drumming evolved from yesterday's drumming, the traditional patterns are applied in different ways. Yesterday's snare drum books prepared students for the music of their time, but as styles have changed and evolved, new books must prepare students for today's music. Ben Hans and John S. Pratt have taken the best of tradition and applied it to modern circumstances. The rudimental tradition is well represented, but so are contemporary applications of that tradition, including a variety of time signatures. This is a book for the present, firmly grounded in the traditions on which the future will be built.

ABOUT THE AUTHORS

Ben Hans

Ben Hans is a musician and music instructor keeping a busy performance schedule throughout the upper Midwest. Ben is an instructor of Percussion, Music Business, Music Reading, Jazz History, the History of Rock Music, and directs the Percussion Ensemble at the Milwaukee Area Technical College, in Milwaukee, Wisconsin. He also instructs more than thirty private music students in his private studio at the Wisconsin Academy of Music. In addition to leading his own jazz trio, Ben performs as a freelance artist. Ben is an adjudicator and charter member of the I.A.T.D. (International Association of Traditional Drummers), and an author, studio musician, proofreader, and freelance editor for the Hal Leonard Corporation. Ben has written four books: *Workin' Drums: 50 Solos for Drum Set, 40 Intermediate Snare Drum Solos, Rudimental Drum Solos for the Marching Snare Drummer,* and *Modern School for Mallet Keyboard Instruments.* Ben is an endorser of Mike Balter Mallets, Istanbul Agop Cymbals, Vic Firth Drumsticks, and is a Yamaha Performing Artist. For updated information, or any comments regarding the content of this book, contact the author at www.benhans.com.

John S. Pratt

John S. (Jack) Pratt, U.S. Army retired, is one of America's greatest rudimentalists and percussion composers. Internationally known for his compositions, teaching, and historic performances, Jack was the instructor of the U.S. Military Academy Band "Hellcats" drum line at West Point. Jack was also an instructor of the Hawthorne Caballeros drum and bugle corps drum line, which won four DCA World Championships and three American Legion National Championships under his direction. Jack founded the International Association of Traditional Drummers (I.A.T.D.) in 2004, which recognizes rudimental drumming excellence, and promotes and preserves the "Traditional" drumming art form. Jack's solo works such as *14 Modern Contest Solos, The Solo Snare Drummer, The New Pratt Book,* and *Rudimental Solos for Accomplished Drummers,* among others, are standard snare drum repertoire. Jack was inducted into the World Drum Corps Hall of Fame, American Patriots Rudimental Drummers Club Hall of Fame, the Percussive Arts Society Hall of Fame, and the New Jersey Drum and Bugle Corps Hall of Fame.

ACKNOWLEDGEMENTS

Special thanks to our student models, Brian Feilbach and Sammie Schacht as well as to Dawn Hans, Joan Pratt, and all the great people at Hal Leonard Corporation.

TIPS FOR SUCCESSFUL MUSIC MAKING

- Count aloud while practicing
- Make counting a habit
- Practice daily
- Use a practice journal
- Sight-read often
- Collect technique and drill materials
- Collect and perform solo material
- Perform in group music making
- Study with a drum teacher
- Find a percussion instructor who can teach you all the percussion instruments
- Invest in a quality practice pad
- Find an area in your home to dedicate to practice
- Leave your instrument up, music stand up, and books on the stand ready to practice
- Invest in a quality metronome
- Attend concerts

- Observe professional percussionists, ask questions
- Watch videos of professional percussionists
- Wear hearing protection—earplugs or headphones—when practicing in small spaces or for extended periods
- Obtain recordings of percussion music
- Use the public library as a resource
- Join the Percussive Arts Society (www.pas.org)
- Know you will need a strong "work ethic"; don't procrastinate or be lazy
- Surround yourself with positive influences
- Dedicate yourself to a practice regimen
- Be open to new techniques or musical ideas
- Know that it will take time to become good; no musician was ever made without many years of practice
- Even professionals practice and continue learning
- Be responsible for your own education and success
- Be a musican who plays the drum

MUSIC FUNDAMENTALS

Music: The combination of tones using basic elements such as rhythm, melody, harmony, form, and timbre in an artistic or emotional manner.

Written musical notation has evolved through the centuries to document the art of music making. It is important for the student to understand this musical documentation described in symbols called notes. For the purpose of this book, we will concern ourselves with the understanding of rhythmic notation.

BINARY NOTATION DIVISION
DIVISION OF TWO

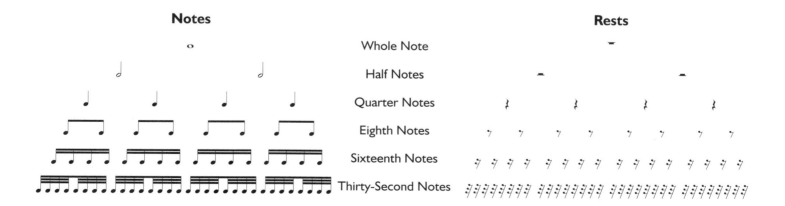

TERNARY NOTATION DIVISION
DIVISION OF THREE

(See Lessons 27 and 28 for information regarding triplets. Return to this page when studying those lessons.)

Half Note Triplets

Quarter Note Triplets

Eighth Note Triplets

Sixteenth Note Triplets
(Sextuplets)

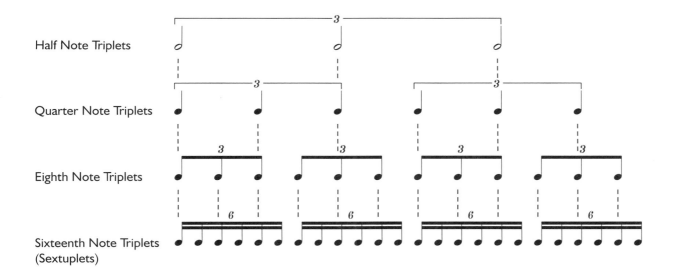

Triplets can be divided into smaller increments just as duple half notes, quarter notes, eighth notes, and sixteenth notes can be subdivided. Practice triplets with a metronome for correct phrasing.

TRUE SEXTUPLET

Based on the triplet, the first, third, and fifth notes are stressed.

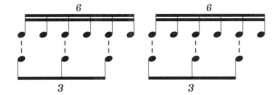

FALSE SEXTUPLET

Based on the duple division of the eighth note, the first and fourth notes are stressed.

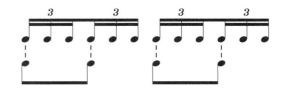

Try this most basic of polyrhythms with two hands. Say "together-right-left-right" and repeat. Also invert the hands for "together-left-right-left." Practice with a metronome to work on the 3:2 polyrhythm. T = Together.

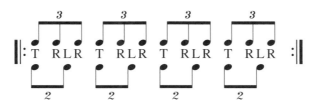

MUSIC TERMINOLOGY AND DESCRIPTIONS

Time Signature: **4/4** Top number tells the number of counts (beats) in each measure.

Bottom number tells what kind of note receives the beat/count.

This time signature indicates that there are:

4/4 4 counts in each measure

The quarter note receives one beat (count)

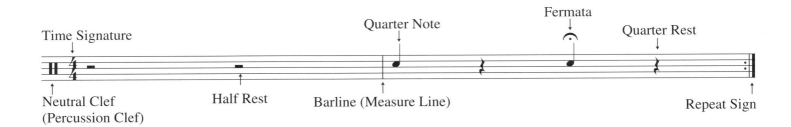

Barline (Measure Line): Divides each measure and resets counting.

Double Barline (one thick, one thin): Signifies the end of a piece of music.

Fermata: To hold out

Measure (Bar): Unit of metrical length of music counting.

Metronome: Device that measures tempo in beats per minute (bpm)

Metronome Marking: The suggested tempo marking at the beginning of a piece of music.

Neutral Clef (Percussion Clef): Musical clef of two vertical lines designating non-pitched percussion instruments.

Polyrhythm: The simultaneous occurrence of two separate or differing rhythm pulses.

Repeat Sign: Signifies the repetition of a phrase or section. Repeat back to the beginning or to the repeat sign facing the opposite direction.

Staff: The grid of lines and spaces that notes are written and read upon.

Tempo: Rate of speed at which music is played.

Thin Double Barline: Signifies the end of a major section of music.

Tempo terms used in this book:

Largo: slow and stately

Andante: at a walking speed, moderately slow

Moderato: at a moderate speed

Allegreto: lively, moderately fast, slower than Allegro

Allegro: quickly, fast

Alla Marcia: in the style and tempo of a march

Presto: very fast or rapid

SNARE DRUM AND STICK DESCRIPTION

Obtain a pair of equally weighted and straight drumsticks. Quality drumsticks will assist you in developing your hands. Unbalanced or misweighted pairs of sticks will feel funny in your hands and hinder your equal hand development. A quality drumstick will roll across a table evenly, and equally paired sticks will have a very similar pitch when tapped with another stick. For the beginner we suggest an SD1, 2B, or comparable drumstick. Find sticks that feel good in your hands. There are many different types of drumsticks. As you build up your musical "chops" you will expand your stick collection for different styles of music. A stick bag (or carry case) and practice pad are recommended for all percussionists.

PARTS OF THE DRUMSTICK

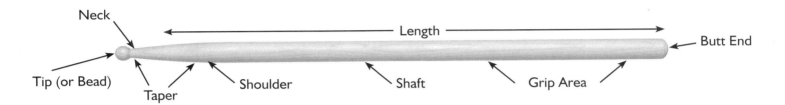

PARTS OF THE SNARE DRUM

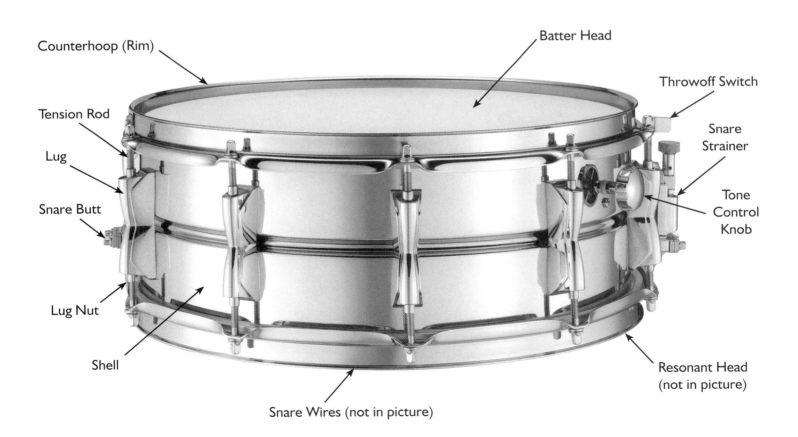

TYPES OF SNARE DRUMS

There are many sizes of snare drums for various uses. Snare drum shells can be manufactured of metal or wood. As you progress in your studies, you may find the need to use or acquire different instruments for different musical situations. Depending upon the style of music you are playing or at the conductor's request, you will eventually find yourself performing on a variety of snare drums and using a variety of sizes of drumsticks. Different circumferences and depths of snare drums (example: 14" circumference x 5.5" depth) in combination with head choice will provide a variety of pitch and tuning possibilities. Here are some common sizes and types of snare drums.

14" X 4" Copper Shell Snare Drum

14" X 5.5" Steel Shell Concert Snare Drum

14" X 6.5" Wood (Maple) Concert Snare Drum

14" X 12" Field Drum (Traditional Parade Drum with Mylar Head)

14" X 12" Marching Drum (High-Tensioned Parade Drum with Kevlar Head**)**

DRUM TUNING

An essential step in maintaining your snare drum is learning how to tune it. The snare drum is a relative-pitch instrument. Drums are tuned with the drum key (or tension key, see below).

Start with the batter head. Tune each area of the drum near the tension rod to the same pitch. Snare drums usually have 8 or 10 tension rods but some vintage and student snare drums have 6. Tap the head nearest the tension rod with your finger or a drumstick to find the fundamental pitch, then obtain the same pitch at each area of the head at the tension rod. When putting on a new drumhead it is recommended to use cross-tensioning tuning. When the new head is seated properly on the drum, clockwise tuning can fine-tune your drum.

To tune the resonant (bottom) head, place a drumstick under the snare wires to separate the snare wires from the resonant head while tuning the head. Use care not to damage the snare wires while tuning the resonant head. The resonant head is thin, so be careful not to tear or dent this head while tuning. Again, obtain the same pitch at each tension rod. A lower pitch at even one point will make the drum ring longer than wanted.

Experiment with tuning your drum. Tune low, tune high. Find the sound that you like. Most orchestral and marching drummers prefer a crisp, higher tone from their snare drums. If you don't like the sound you are getting from your instrument, release all tension on the head and try again. If you tune too high, you can choke off the natural, resonating sound of the instrument. Use the snare strainer adjustment knob to adjust the tension of the snare wires. Make sure that your wires are not pulled unevenly to one side of the resonant head. This can affect the sound of your drum.

Be cautious that you do not tune so high with force that you damage the lugs. However, if this happens, remember you can replace all the parts of the drum except the shell. Lugs and tension rods occasionally wear out or strip out. With the correct replacement parts and a bit of patience, reheading, tuning, and repair can be done at home in a few minutes. If needed, take the drum to your local drum shop for help if you have trouble finding or replacing the correct parts.

Although you could use a chromatic tuning device to precisely obtain a specified pitch, it is best to train your ears to obtain a good sound. Do not fear taking your snare drum to your drum instructor and asking for help.

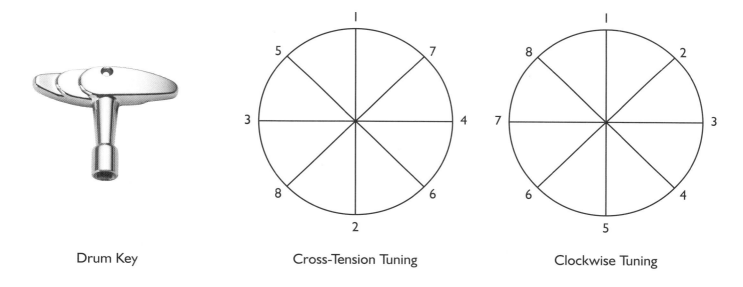

Drum Key   Cross-Tension Tuning   Clockwise Tuning

For tips on maintaining, tuning, and caring for your drum, the book *Drum Tuning* by Scott Schroedl (Hal Leonard Corporation HL06620060) is recommended. This book/CD package provides sound sources and gives tips on drumhead choice and drum maintenance.

MATCHED GRIP

Matched Grip is the most widely used and taught of the two distinct snare drum grips. Matched Grip is often used because both handholds are identical (but mirrored). The main reasons for the popularity of this grip is that it is easier for the beginning drummer to learn, as both hands are the same, and that it is easily transferable to most percussion instruments that use sticks or mallets. Therefore, it is most often taught initially, and sometimes solely, to beginning and intermediate percussionists.

The Traditional Grip is another way to hold the drumsticks. (For a discussion of Traditional Grip, see the next page.) As you progress to the intermediate and professional level, you will find that there are various approaches to grip. Remember that you want to have a stick grip that provides tension-free playing that can last a lifetime. Tension is to be avoided and can cause injury.

Within the Matched Grip there are three basic variations: German, French, and American. One should be aware of all these types of matched grip, as each produces different sounds. However, for performance on snare drum, we will focus on the German Matched Grip, which is formally called German Timpani Grip.

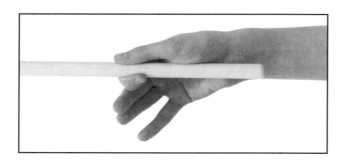

1. Hold the stick a third of the way up from the butt end between the pad of the thumb and the first knuckle from the tip of the index finger (forefinger). This is called the fulcrum (pivot point).

> **Tip:** Have some openness in the gap of space between the thumb and index finger; some call this "open fulcrum." Let your hand hang at your side and see how it is curved in its relaxed state. Keep this relaxed, tension-free shape in the hand when playing.

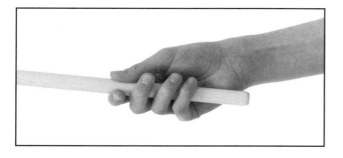

2. Wrap the fingers around the shaft (gripping area) of the stick gently. Fingers should be touching the stick in a relaxed manner. Maintain the natural shape of the hand.

> **Tip:** When playing, do not allow the stick to slide up into or past the second joint of the index finger. This will cause unwanted tension in the hand. Sometimes called "collapsed fulcrum," this will force the remaining fingers off the stick and "thin out" your sound.

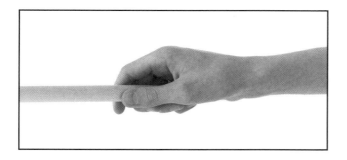

3. Let the stick fall through the hand naturally with a bit of the butt-end visible from the end of the hand. Move the wrist in a waving motion (referred to as the "bye-bye" motion by some). Remain relaxed and free of tension. Make an up-down motion with the wrist—palm flat, straight up and down. Avoid what some refer to as "the slice"—an angled stroke.

> **Tip:** Hold the wrist straight up in the air. Move the hand at the wrist, flopping back and forth. Notice the natural closing of the finger muscles as the hand flops backwards at the wrist. Notice where the thumb falls. In a relaxed hand, you have the thumb meeting the first joint of (or directly above) the index finger. You will have to physically move the thumb up at an angle to the second joint or beyond the index finger (which is a "collapsed fulcrum" with no open space between the thumb and hand). This creates tension and should be avoided.

TRADITIONAL GRIP

The Traditional Grip for snare drum is less often taught today, but it is still used and is the preferred snare drum grip by many jazz drummers and drum corps snare lines. Traditional Grip was used less and less through the last half of the 20th century as it comes from the period of drumming when a snare drum was worn on a sling across the chest. Today's percussionists are generally playing a drum that is flat, which removes the angled/slung drum and the need for the Traditional Grip. However, many percussionists enjoy using Traditional Grip, and it is worthwhile learning it. It is recommended that any serious student of percussion eventually learn the Traditional Grip, if not for individual use, then at least for the passing down of this technique. Traditional Grip is a hot-button issue among some percussionists. Many articles have been written regarding the relevance of this ancient grip.

Remember, it is the sound that counts. Technique is the way to produce sound. Decide for yourself which technique works best for you. With the exception of the marching band, where there is a uniform decision throughout the snare drum line of using Matched or Traditional Grip, as long as the music is played correctly, the choice of grip does not matter. Choose the one that works best for you.

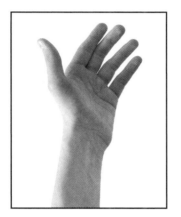

1. Using the left hand only, let your arm hang at your side completely free of tension. Keeping the natural curl of the muscles of your hand, bring the arm up at the elbow at approximately a 90-degree angle.

Tip: Try rotating your hand side to side, using the thumb to gently tap the drum to simulate the stroke.

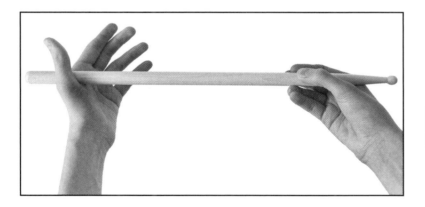

2. Place the stick in the "webbing" (1st Dorsal Interosseous and knuckles) of the hand with the butt end of the stick several inches out from the back of your hand. This will become the fulcrum or pivot point.

Tip: Keep the thumb straight. It can touch the index finger, but should not curl up.

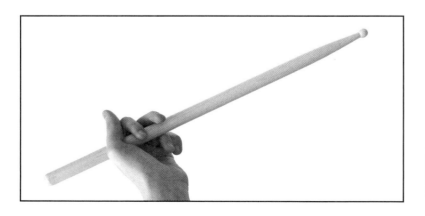

3. Bring the index finger up over the stick and lock the stick into place. The middle finger rides up and over against the stick and supports the motion of the stroke. The two remaining fingers curl up and support the stick, with the ring finger touching the bottom of the drumstick at the knuckle/cuticle area.

Tip: Avoid letting the index and middle fingers flop off the stick while playing, slapping the stick down against your ring finger. Ouch!

Tip: When playing, use a motion similar to turning a doorknob. Jim Sewrey likes to describe the motion of the wrist turn as that of holding a paper cup of coffee and pouring it out over the back of the hand. You can also think of the Traditional Grip as a Matched Grip upside down. Switch back and forth from what is called back sticking to see the similarities in the grips.

HAND POSITION
From the Top, Front, and Side

Hold the sticks in a triangular pattern with a 60 to 90 degree angle in front of you.

Front-view position

Side-view position

RUDIMENTS

Drum rudiments are patterns unique to the art of drumming that have been passed down for centuries from one drummer to another, aurally at first by onomatopoeia (the naming of something by the vocal imitation of the sound it produces), and eventually through written notation. Initially used as military calls and signals, rudiments today are most often used as musical expression in music and used in rudimental drum solos. A thorough background of rudimental study and technique is encouraged for all percussionists.

There is a storied history of opinion among band directors and percussionists regarding the importance and use of the rudiments in certain styles of music making though the years. This is especially prevalent in the approach of the orchestral snare drum player, as the player may not encounter any rudiments during the performance of many pieces in orchestral snare drum literature. It is true that while playing percussion instruments, there will be instances where no rudimental drumming styles or techniques will be used. Nevertheless, the authors highly encourage the practice and continuous study of rudimental drumming, as the contrary is also true. The percussionist will find a use for rudimental technique on many of the other percussion instruments in many situations.

It is the authors' belief, shared by scores of percussionists, that a solid foundation of rudimental study will be of great help to the student and assist in music making. The snare drum is an old and noble instrument; take the responsibility to study it and pass on the rich heritage and art form of your instrument.

FIVE BASIC STROKES

In this book, we will utilize the following five basic strokes. Although the names of the strokes can vary from teacher to teacher, the concepts below formulate most of the primary sounds you will produce. Much of your performance, as well as many of the drumming rudiments, will consist of one or a combination of these strokes. Knowing and performing the following strokes well will provide an important practical basis of your future performance.

Full Stroke (Rebound Stroke)

Hold the stick approximately 8 to 12 inches above the drum. In a combination of wrist and finger motion, propel the stick downward toward the drum. After contact is made, let the stick and wrist naturally rebound and return the energy of the stroke back to the up position.

Down Stroke

In the same manner of the full stroke, propel the stick down toward the drum. After striking the drum, gently firm up the fingers/hand slightly to prevent the stick from returning the energy from the stroke upwards, keeping the tip of the stick close to the drumhead (approximately 1 inch).

Up Stroke

From a very low position (the end of the down stroke position), use finger and wrist action to strike the drumhead in a reverse or pull-out motion. The stroke is played as the wrist is rising to return to the up position. This stroke will take some diligent practice but will be of great value to you.

Tap Stroke

The tap stroke starts from a low position and returns to a low position. It is a short, low, quick tap used for many playing situations.

Multiple Stroke

The multiple stroke (also called the multiple-bounce stroke) is an application of the down stroke. Immediately after making the down stroke, apply a temporary fulcrum and finger pressure to bounce the stick off of the head, achieving three or more bounces. This stroke will be of much importance to develop the concert (orchestral) roll.

STICKING PATTERNS

Practice tips: Below are some sticking patterns to use for warming up. Use each of the five basic strokes while practicing these patterns. Work through each example 20 or more times.

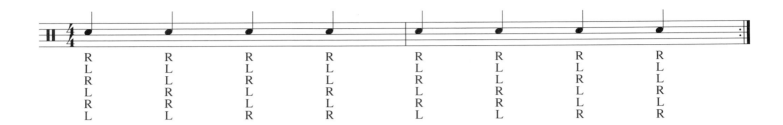

Sticking Systems

Drummers use two basic sticking systems. The first is the alternating system, where the drummer simply plays R L R L etc. consistently through each rhythm and pattern, even over rests. Many rudimental-based performers use this system. This system is generally started with the right hand, but for dexterity should also be practiced with a left-hand lead.

A system preferred by many percussionists is the natural sticking system or Straight System, named after early 20th-century drummer and author Edward B. Straight. In the Straight System, the right hand leads and is favored on strong beats while the left hand plays the weak beats. The right hand dominates downbeats and commences each new measure.

Edward B. Straight was not opposed to the alternating sticking used in rudimental drumming. In fact, Straight was one of the original 13 N.A.R.D. (National Association of Rudimental Drummers) members, founded in Chicago in 1933. Straight's books, *The Straight System of Modern Drumming: the Natural Way to Play Drums*, *Analysis of 6/8 Time*, and *Straight's Modern Syncopated Rhythms for Drums* are fascinating studies of our drumming heritage.

We recommend that students work with each sticking system, applying them when appropriate. Much rudimental drumming includes written stickings, which should be followed. You many find suggested stickings in your drum parts, and these should also be followed. If you perform with marching-percussion units, stickings are important to achieve a uniform visual look for the snare drum line. For orchestral playing, many prefer the Straight System for its uniformity of sound and simplicity of performance. Remember, concert band leaders and orchestral conductors care most about correct articulation and rhythmic precision, not about which sticking you are using.

How to Practice

Regular practice is needed to grow as a musician. Even the great players must practice often to keep their skills sharp. Try to retain a set practice schedule to help make music an everyday part of your life. The best part of music is that you can never become "too good" or "know it all." There is always room for growth.

Practice is needed every day to become the best musician you can be. Each day and week, you will be building on the improvements you have made before. Thirty to sixty minutes a day is all that is needed for the beginner. That is only the amount of time it takes to watch one television show.

Use the Practice Journal at the end of this book to track your practice. Constant and daily practice will cause the biggest improvement in your playing. Without constant practice, it is impossible to improve on your instrument! Remember, practicing is merely consistent repetition and eventual mastery of a given task. New things will become familiar and easier with practice. Start building habits that will make you the best you can be. It's all up to you; you can take music as far as you want as long as you continue to practice and have a positive attitude.

If you practice every day, you can take your music as far as you want.

LESSON 1
QUARTER NOTES ♩ AND QUARTER RESTS 𝄽

Practice tips: Count out loud when practicing. For increased technical facility, lesson examples throughout this book should be practiced with * right-hand lead and left-hand lead in alternating (hand-to-hand) sticking, ** as well as with natural (Straight System) sticking.

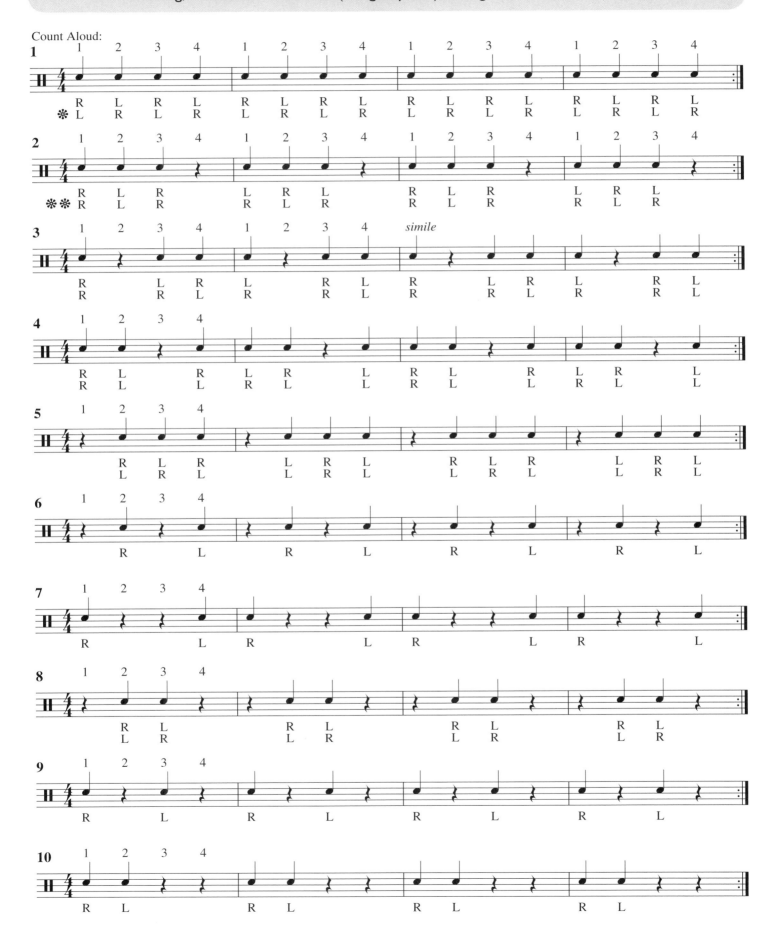

LESSON 2

HALF NOTES ♩   WHOLE NOTES ○
HALF RESTS -   WHOLE RESTS -

Practice tips: Count aloud when practicing. You will see half notes and whole notes more often when playing bass drum, timpani, and other percussion instruments, especially when working with winds and strings.

LESSON 3
EIGHTH NOTES ♫ AND QUARTER NOTES ♩

Practice tips: Keep a practice journal. Practice regularly with a metronome. Count aloud when practicing. Count eighth notes as "1 and 2 and" or "1 an 2 an" (+ = "and"). When using alternating sticking, if the exercise ends on an R, repeat with a left-hand lead. Practice in alternating sticking with right-hand and left-hand leads as well as with natural (Straight System) sticking. Check your grip. Play in a relaxed manner.

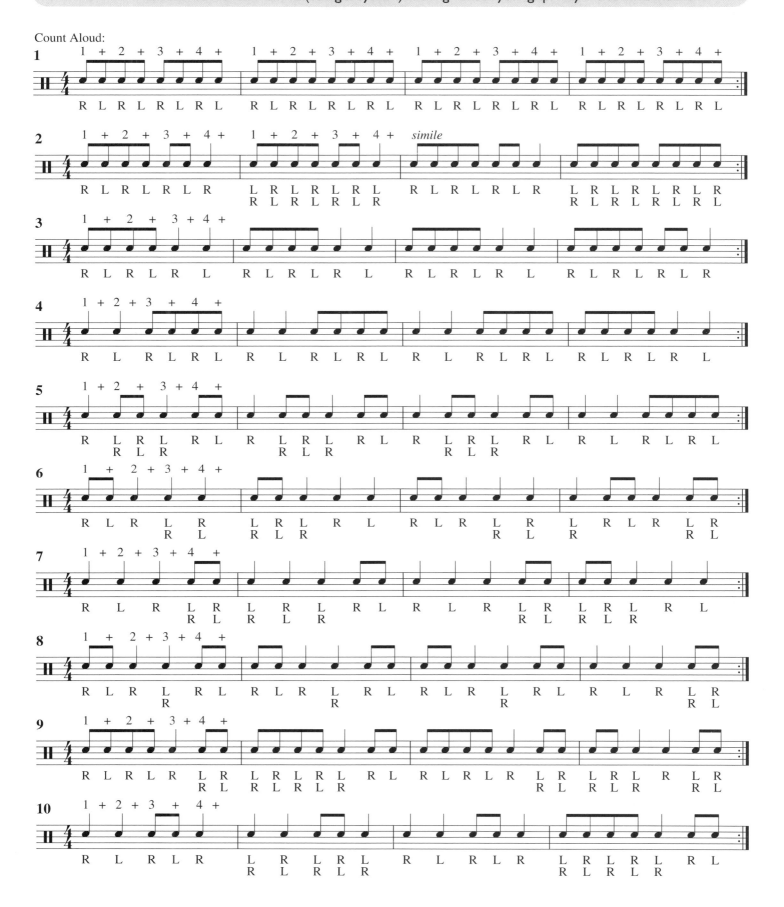

LESSON 4
STUDIES IN EIGHTH NOTES AND QUARTER NOTES

Dynamics: Intensity of sound
f = *forte* = loud
p = *piano* = soft

Study I

Study II

LESSON 5
16-MEASURE STUDIES IN QUARTER NOTES AND EIGHTH NOTES

Crescendo
Decrescendo (or Diminuendo)

Dynamics: Intensity of sound
ff = *fortissimo* = very loud
pp = *pianissimo* = very soft

LESSON 6
EIGHTH NOTES ♪ AND EIGHTH RESTS ♪

Practice tips: Practice regularly and often. Count aloud when practicing. Count eighth notes as "1 and 2 and" or "1 an 2 an" (+ = "and"). Play with the metronome at 60 bpm (beats per minute) and increase at intervals of 10 bpm with both alternating and natural stickings.

LESSON 7
MORE EIGHTH NOTES ♪ AND EIGHTH RESTS ７

Practice tips: Practice regularly; consistent practice will make you better. Two eighth rests ７７ = one quarter rest 𝄽.

LESSON 8
16-MEASURE STUDIES IN 4/4

sempre = throughout

Study I

Study II

Study III

ÉTUDE I

Dynamics: Intensity of sound
mf = *mezzo forte* = medium loud
mp = *mezzo piano* = medium soft

Practice tips: 4/4 is used so often in music that it is referred to as "common time" and is often marked with a **C** sign.

LESSON 9
INTRODUCTION TO 2/4 TIME

♩ = 2 Counts in measure
♩ = Gets the beat (count)

Practice tips: 2/4 time has two quarter-note beats in each measure. Count aloud ("1 and 2 and").
*"Syncopation" occurs when a strong beat is moved to a weak beat and creates rhythmic tension;
i.e., when a note is moved to an upbeat ("and") and receives the stress in place of the downbeat.

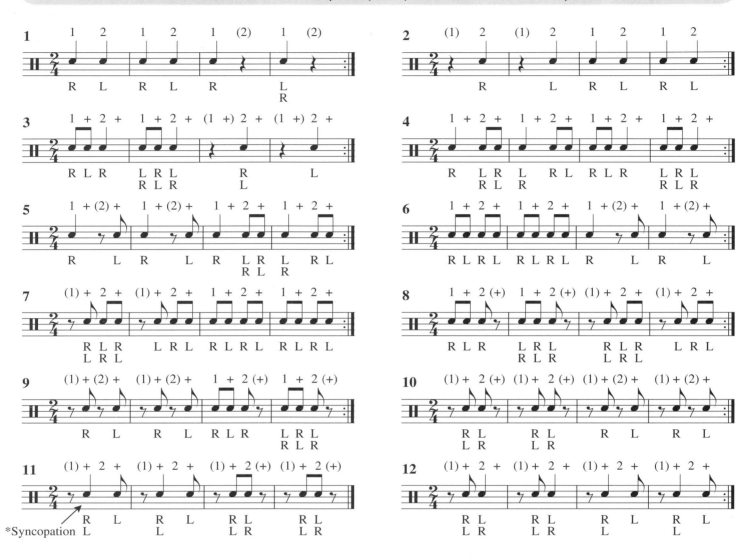

16-Measure Studies in 2/4

Study I

Moderato

∕ = repeat the previous measure

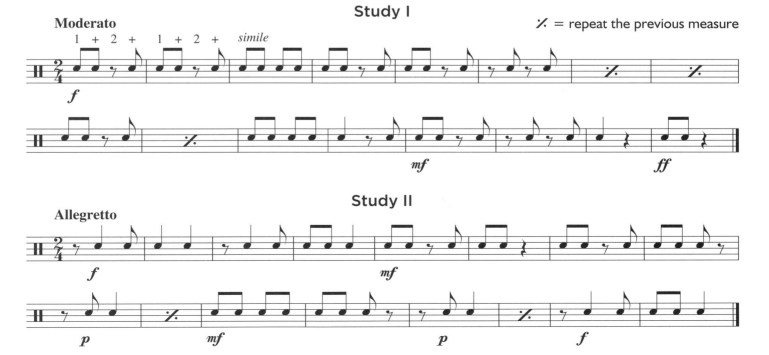

Study II

Allegretto

ÉTUDE II

mp – *mf* = change dynamics on repeat

Two-measure repeat = repeat the two previous measures

First ending – take on first repeat only

Second ending – take on second repeat only

LESSON 10
ACCENT STUDIES

Practice tips: An essential articulation in snare drum playing is the use of accented notes. Accents (>) are notes that receive stress and emphasis. Play a firm downstroke from a higher stick height to achieve a louder sound on accented notes. After you've completed the alternating sticking studies, replay the examples below with the sticking R L R R – L R L L—the Single Paradiddle Rudiment. Also practice from snare drum technique books that feature accents. The authors recommend *Syncopation* by Ted Reed and *Accents and Rebounds* by George Lawrence Stone.

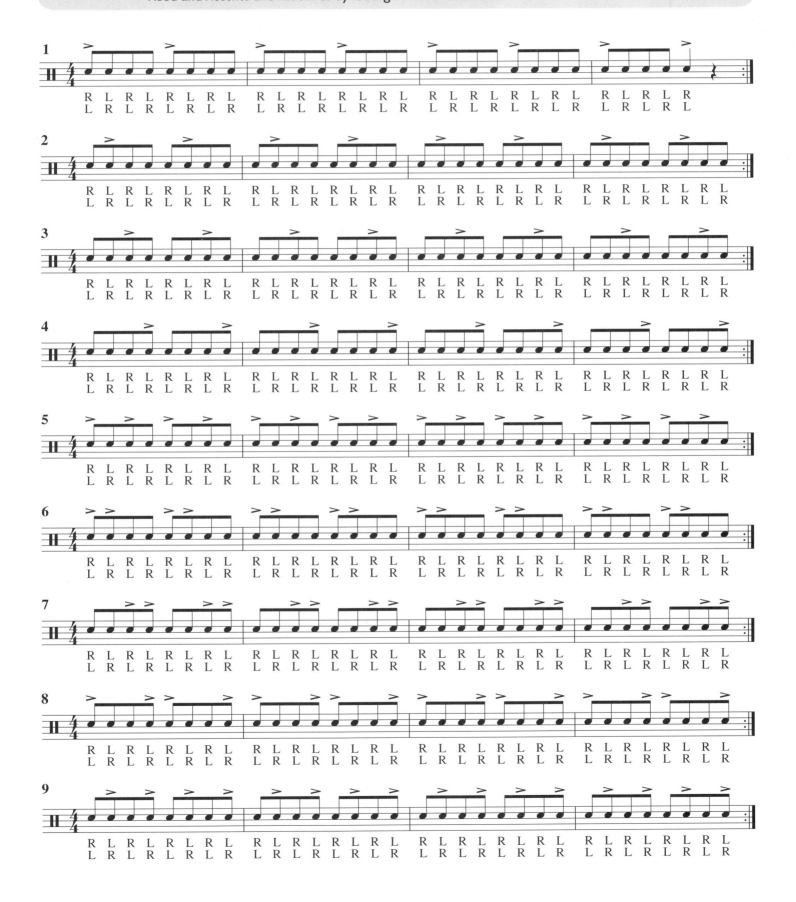

LESSON 11
SIXTEENTH NOTES ♫

Practice tips: Count aloud—"1 e and ah, 2 e and ah"—for rhythmic precision. Practice regularly with a metronome. Practice with right-hand and left-hand alternating lead as well as natural sticking. Be sure to observe the time signature switch to 4/4 in the last three examples.

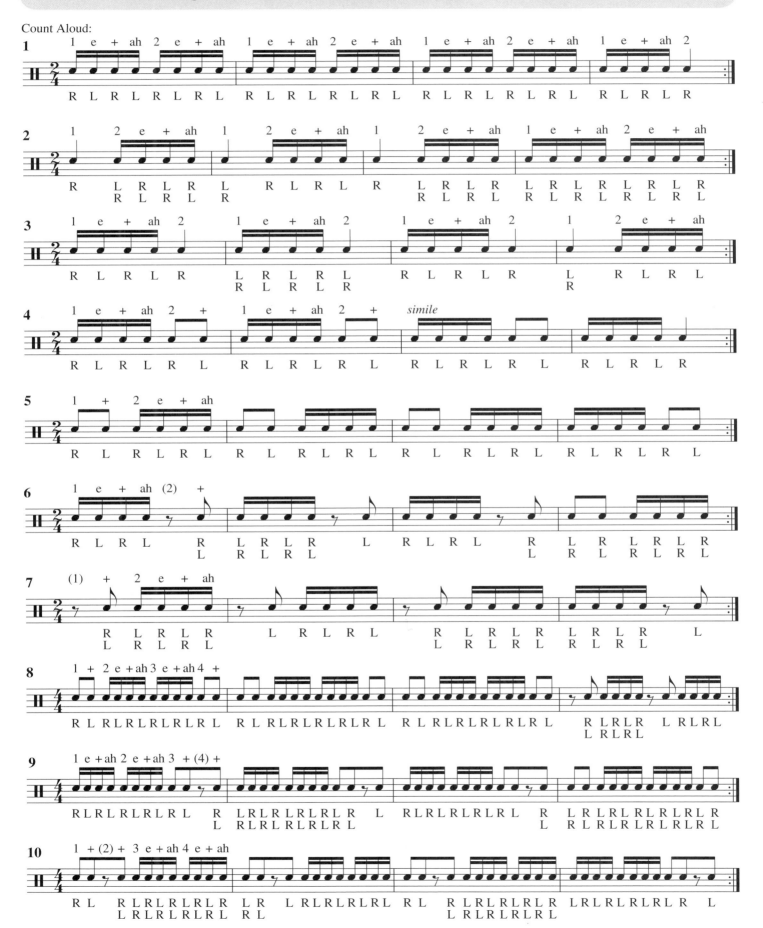

LESSON 12
EIGHTH-NOTE AND SIXTEENTH-NOTE GROUPS &

Practice tips: Count aloud—"1 e and ah, 2 e and ah"—for rhythmic precision. Practice regularly with a metronome. Practice with right-hand and left-hand alternating lead and natural sticking. Practice repeatedly so that you recognize the two different eighth-note and sixteenth-note groups.

LESSON 13
STUDIES USING SIXTEENTH-NOTE RHYTHMS

sfz = *sforzando*: perform with stress or sudden emphasis

fp = *forte-piano*: begin strongly at *forte* with immediate reduction to *piano*

dim. = *diminuendo*: gradually softer

cres. = *crescendo*: gradually louder

∧ = *marcato*: use a strong, heavy accent

ÉTUDE III

Practice tips: Count aloud while practicing. Practice a few measures at a time. Become familiar with these rhythms, as you will see them often. Observe dynamic changes.

ÉTUDE IV

x = Play on outer rim
● = Play on head 1/2 way to edge of drum

𝄋 = Sign

D.S. = Dal Segno = "From the Sign," i.e., return to the Sign

⊕ = Coda sign

D.S. al Coda = Return to the Sign, play to Coda sign, advance to Coda (ending)

Practice tips: Playing halfway between the edge and center of the drumhead produces a different timbre (quality of sound). Explore the different sounds you can coax from your instrument.

LESSON 14
INTRODUCTION TO 3/4 TIME

3 Counts in measure

♩ Gets the beat (count)

Practice tips: Work with a metronome for correct phrasing of 3/4 rhythms. For additional study, on a sheet of staff paper, compose your own 16-measure exercises in 3/4.

Count Aloud:

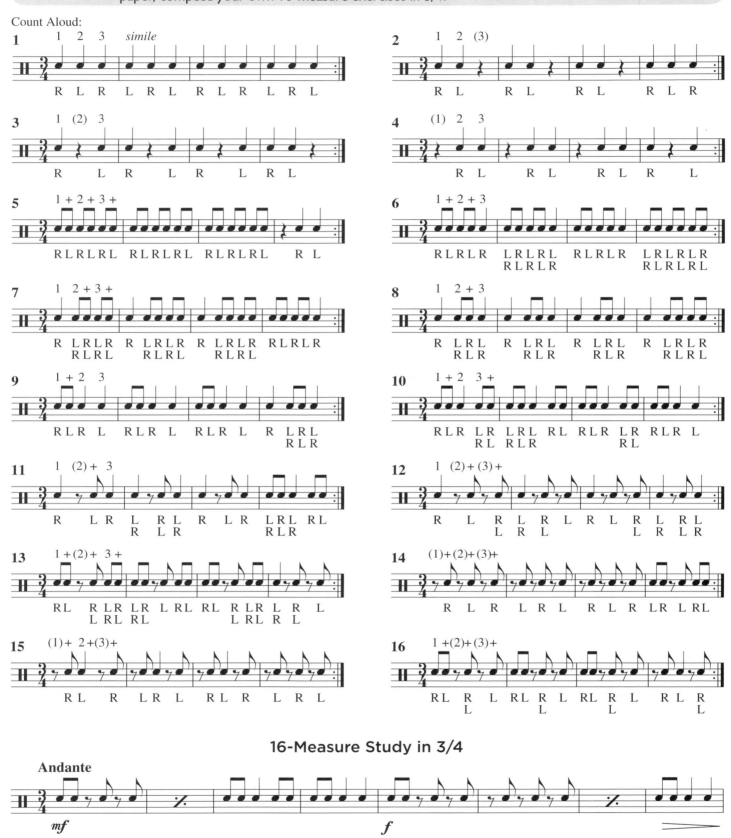

16-Measure Study in 3/4

LESSON 15
SIXTEENTH NOTES IN 3/4

Count Aloud:

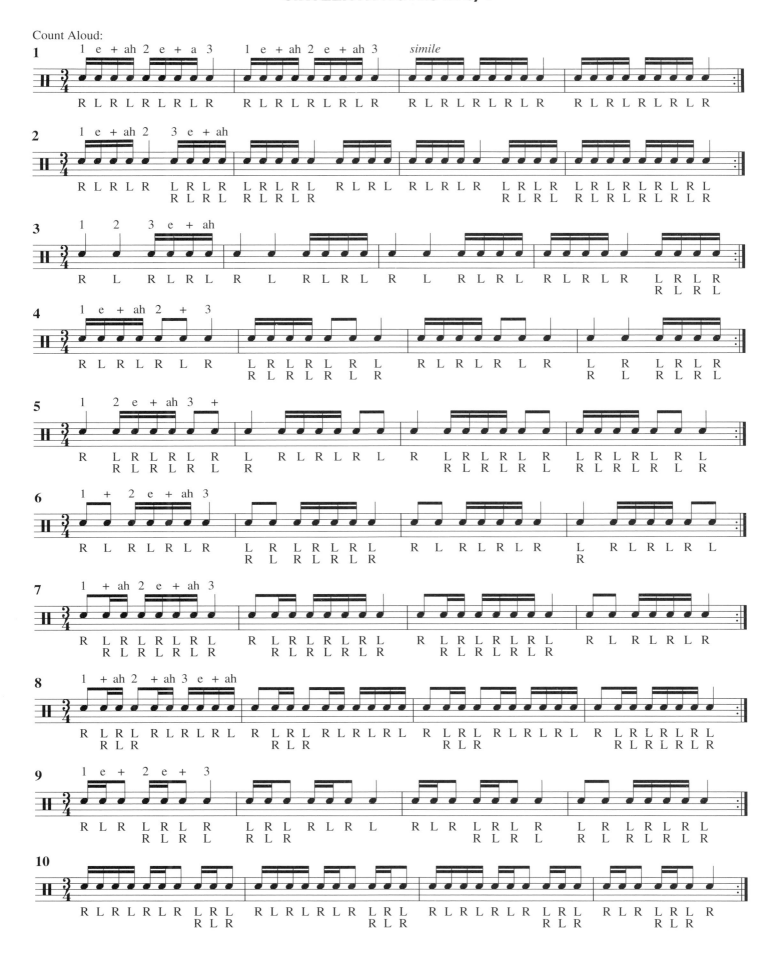

LESSON 16
16-MEASURE STUDIES IN 3/4

Study I

Study II

Study III

DUET IN 3/4

D.C. = Da Capo = return to beginning
Fine = End of a piece of music
D.C. al Fine = return to beginning and
play until Fine

LESSON 17
INTRODUCTION TO 5/4

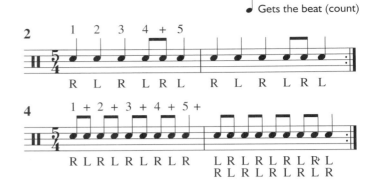

5 Counts in measure
♩ Gets the beat (count)

Count Aloud:

1
1 2 3 4 5

R L R L R   L R L R L

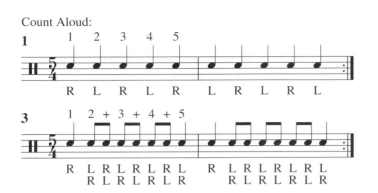

2
1 2 3 4 + 5

R L R L RL   R L R L RL

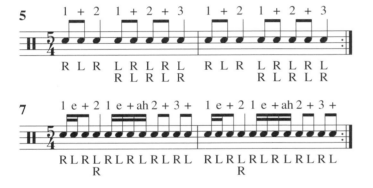

3
1 2 + 3 + 4 + 5

R L R L R L R L
R L R L R L R

R L R L R L R L
R L R L R L R

4
1 + 2 + 3 + 4 + 5 +

R L R L R L R L R   L R L R L R L R L
R L R L R L R L R

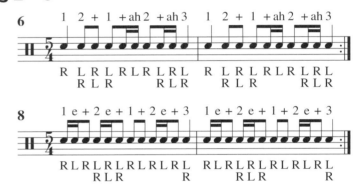

Practice tips: Musicians often group measures of 5/4 into smaller groups of 2 + 3 (counted 1 2 1 2 3) or 3 + 2 (counted 1 2 3 1 2). Use the counting system that works best for you.

Counting 2 + 3

5
1 + 2   1 + 2 + 3

R L R   L R L R L
R L R L R

R L R   L R L R L
R L R L R

6
1 2 + 1 + ah 2 + ah 3

R L R L R L R L R L
R L R   R L R

R L R L R L R L R L
R L R   R L R

7
1 e + 2 1 e + ah 2 + 3 +

R L R L R L R L R L R L
R

R L R L R L R L R L R L
R

8
1 e + 2 e + 1 + 2 + 3

R L R L R L R L R L R L
R L R   R

R L R L R L R L R L R L
R L R   R

Counting 3 + 2

9
1 + 2 + 3 + 1 e + 2

R L R L R L R L R L
R

R L R L R L R L R L
R

10
1 e + 2 e + 3   1 e + 2 +

R L R L R L R L R L R L
R L R   R L R

R L R L R L R L R L R L
R L R   R L R

11
1 + ah (2) + 3 + 1 + ah (2) +

R L R   L R L R L R   L
R L   R L

R L R   L R L R L R   L
R L   R L

12
1 + (2) + (3) + (1) + ah (2) + ah

R L   R   L   R L   R L R L   R   L   R L   R L
L   L

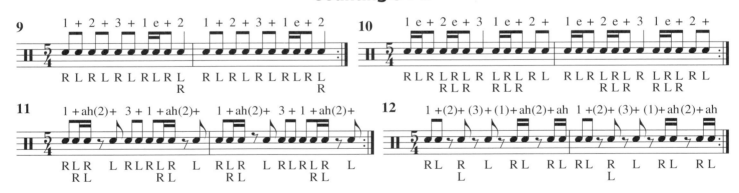

Study

Andante

𝆑 *sempre*

LESSON 18
STUDIES IN 5/4

Study I

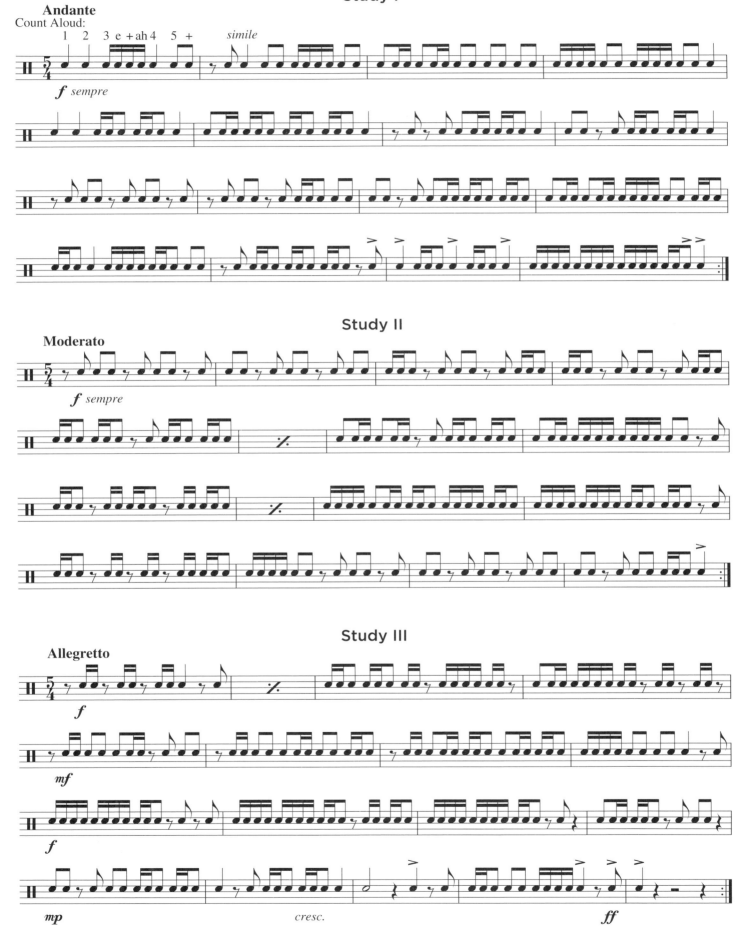

Study II

Study III

DUET IN 5/4

G.P. = General Pause
(Grand Pause)

LESSON 19

DOTTED HALF NOTES 𝅗𝅥.,
DOTTED QUARTER NOTES ♩., AND TIED NOTES ♩‿♩

Practice tips: Composers often use dots and ties to extend note values. Because the snare drum has a short, staccato sound, the player cannot hold a dotted note or tied notes the way a wind instrument or vocalist can (unless you roll; more on that later). When playing tied or dotted notes, the snare drummer must play the initial attack stroke and then count the remainder of the note value. A dot (.) increases the value of the original note by half. Phrasing is similar to a rest; the snare drummer must count, but not play, the additional duration of the note. As always, counting aloud when practicing is a must.

A tie (‿) sustains a note by connecting another note to it. The snare drummer must play the first note and count the value of the note that is tied to it. Essentially, on snare drum, the second (tied) note is treated as a rest.

Because of the snare drum's staccato sound, the same rhythm can be notated several ways. The following notations must be understood.

LESSON 20
STUDIES IN DOTTED AND TIED NOTES WITH SYNCOPATIONS

Practice tips: Practice two measures at a time. Count aloud. Practice with a metronome. Count syncopated measures carefully when the beat emphasis shifts to the weak beat.

Study I

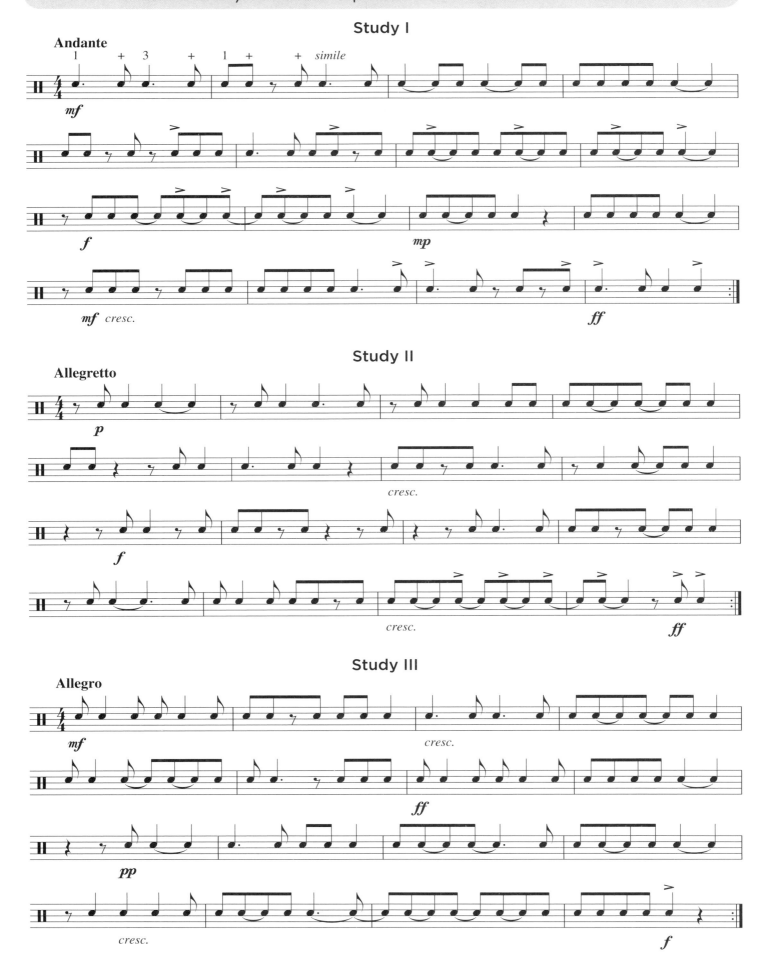

ÉTUDE V

Practice tips: Count throughout this etude to attain correct placement of the tied and dotted notes. Practice with a metronome for rhythmic precision.

LESSON 21
SIXTEENTH-NOTE GROUPS

Practice tips: Count these rhythms, which use sixteenth rests and syncopations, aloud. These rhythms appear often in music, so become very familiar with them. Review this page often. Practice with a metronome for correct rhythmic articulation.

Two-Note Groups

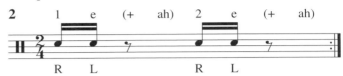

 = Sixteenth Rest

 Dotted Eighth Note = Three Sixteenth Notes

Three-Note Groups
with one sixteenth rest

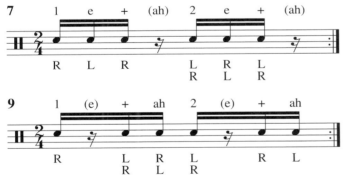

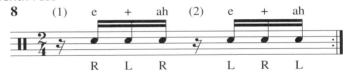

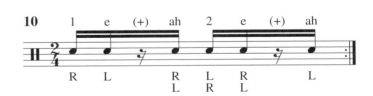

Additional Syncopated Groups

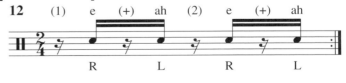

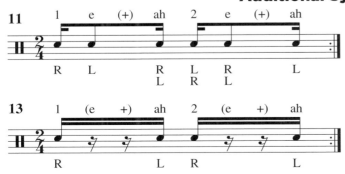

LESSON 22
SIXTEENTH-NOTE GROUP EXERCISES

Practice tips: Count these syncopated groups aloud—"1 e and ah, 2 e and ah"—for rhythmic precision. Practice with a metronome. Practice with right-hand and left-hand alternating lead and natural sticking. Practice repeatedly so that you recognize the sixteenth-note groups.

LESSON 23
STUDIES USING SIXTEENTH-NOTE GROUPS AND SIXTEENTH RESTS

Study I

Study II

Study III

DUET IN 2/4

ÉTUDE VI

Dynamics: Intensity of sound
fff = *fortississimo* = very, very loud
ppp = *pianississimo* = very, very soft

Practice tips: This étude features syncopated sixteenth-note rhythms. Be sure to count all the rhythms while practicing this étude. Keep the quarter-note pulse throughout.

Allegretto ♩ = 108

LESSON 24
INTRODUCTION TO 3/8

3 Counts in measure
♪ Gets the beat (count)

Practice tips: When counting in 3/8, use the eighth note as the common pulse. Sixteenth notes should be counted "1 and 2 and 3 and." A dotted quarter note takes up an entire measure.

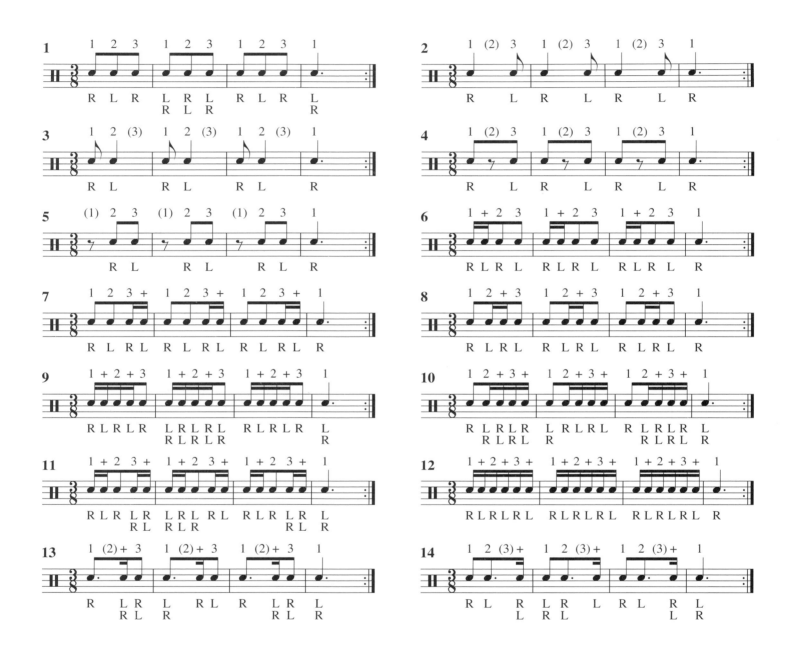

Study

LESSON 25
INTRODUCTION TO 6/8

6 Counts in measure

♪ Gets the beat (count)

Practice tips: When counting in 6/8, use the eighth note as the common pulse. Sixteenth notes should be counted "1 and 2 and 3 and 4 and 5 and 6 and." A dotted quarter note takes up half a measure (three eighth notes).

An interesting suggestion by Edward B. Straight in his books *The Straight System: The Natural Way to Play Drums* and *Analysis of 6/8 Time* is to play 6/8 rhythms in repeated R L R R L R sticking patterns. Experiment with this sticking idea in addition to the right-hand and left-hand alternating sticking. Straight's sticking may work for you.

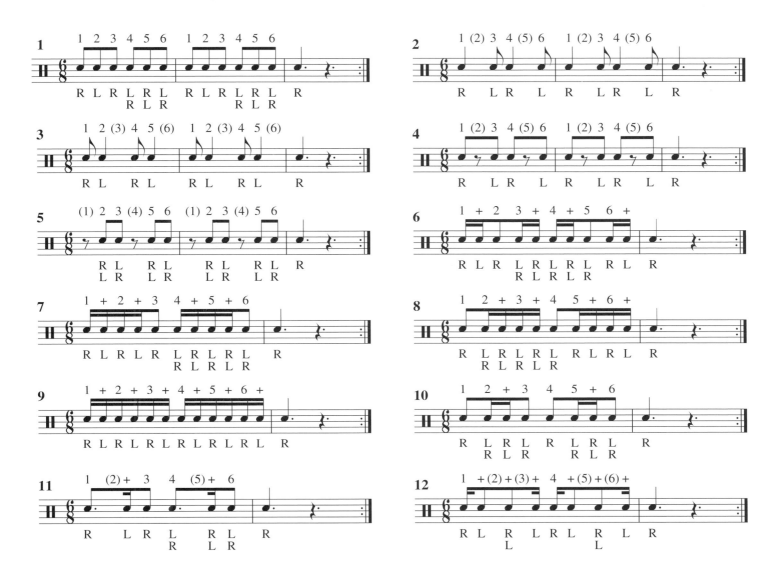

Study

Moderato

mf sempre

LESSON 26
STUDIES IN 3/8 AND 6/8

Study I

LESSON 27
TRIPLETS

Practice tips: Triplets are divisions of three notes. A triplet will have the number 3 above it. Count aloud "trip-o-let, trip-o-let" to attain the correct feel of the note grouping. While counting, you can substitute the number of the beat on the first note of the triplet (a downbeat or an "and"): "1-o-let, 2-o-let," or "1-trip-let, 2 trip-let," or "1-trip-let, and-trip-let." Some people count "1-ti-ta, 2-ti-ta" or "1-an-ah, 2-an-ah." Use the counting system that works best for you or that your teacher recommends. Practice the exercises below with left-hand lead also. Practice with a metronome to obtain rhythmic accuracy.

Eighth-Note Triplets

Developing Quarter-Note Triplets

Eighth Notes mixed with Eighth-Note Triplets
(use a metronome for rhythmic accuracy)

LESSON 28
SIXTEENTH-NOTE TRIPLETS

Practice tips: Sixteenth-note triplets are created from a triple division of the eighth note. Count aloud and practice these rhythms slowly at first. Practice with left-hand lead as well.

Study in Sixteenth-Note Triplets

Practice tips: Below is an example of the use of sixteenth-note triplets as a rhythmic ostinato (constant repetition of a theme or motive) in Ravel's "Bolero." Obtain a recording of this piece and play along with it.

LESSON 29
INTRODUCTION TO ROLLS
Single-Stroke and Double-Stroke Rolls

Snare drummers use several types of drum rolls. Because the snare drum produces a staccato sound, the roll is the method used to obtain sustained tones on the instrument. Much practice is needed to produce an even, clean-sounding drum roll. With correct technique, as well as consistent and regular practice, you will attain a good roll sound.

SINGLE-STROKE ROLL
The Single-Stroke Roll is an important aspect of drumming. As its name implies, it consists of single strokes, played very, very fast. This is an important rudiment to master as it does not only apply to snare drum but to many other percussion instruments as well. Practice exercises a, b, and c from slow to fast. Exercise c introduces thirty-second notes. Do not tense up when playing fast. Use a full stroke. You will notice that your sticks need to move closer and closer to the drumhead as your speed increases. Avoid tension.

DOUBLE-STROKE ROLL
The Double-Stroke Roll (also called the Long Roll) consists of two strokes per hand movement. Use one wrist stroke to create two notes. The second note will use the fingers to the return the stick to an up position. You want to work toward playing two thirty-second notes with each hand movement. To develop this, try each exercise moving from a to b (to c). Also, try each numbered exercise below without the repeats between examples a and b. Play slowly at first. You should also practice the rudimental breakdown of the Double-Stroke Roll from slow to fast to slow. Make sure each hand is producing equal sounds with notes that are balanced. You will have to work continually with your non-dominant hand to produce an even sound. With practice and dedication, you will accomplish this.

LESSON 29 (continued)

Introduction to Multiple-Bounce Rolls

The Multiple-Bounce Roll (also called the orchestral, press, concert, or buzz roll) is obtained by playing the Multiple-Bounce stroke from hand to hand in a consistent manner. You will need to practice this stroke to obtain a fluid Multiple Bounce. Don't press so hard that you strain your hands or "fuzz out" the tone of the drum with a dead stroke. You want a full sound that will emulate the sound of paper being torn. The Z notation on the stem signifies a Multiple-Bounce stroke.

Preparatory Exercises

Play three to nine bounces per stroke.

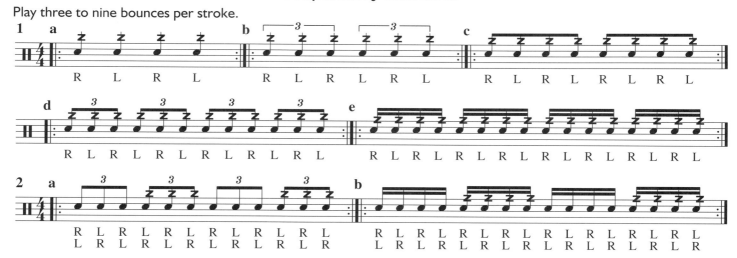

When reading Multiple-Bounce Rolls, identify the note value accompanied by the tied note. This signifies the length of time that a note should be sustained by rolling. With the Multiple-Bounce Roll, the tempo will designate how many hand movements should be used to produce the sustained note. The player must count the duration of the tied note and decide if a duple, triple, or quadruple pulse should be used. Experiment with pulses at different tempos to sustain the following rolls.

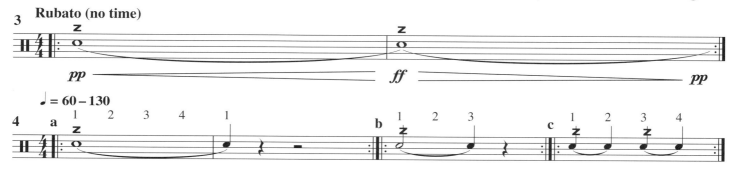

MORE TIPS ON ROLLS

In the Double-Stroke Roll, there will be two bounces per hand movement. The note length will designate how many strokes will be produced for the specific roll rudiment. The player must count the note duration and play the specific number of strokes to obtain the correct roll. Notation will include a tie and the number of slashes on the stem to signify thirty-second notes. The shortest Double-Stroke Roll is the 5-Stroke Roll, explained in the next lesson.

One must understand what style of music is being performed in each situation and choose the proper type of roll. Snare drum music is often notated with slashes on the stem instead of a Z, so one must understand the style of the music. Intermediate and advanced players must also be aware of drum and stick choices to correctly play music in the appropriate manner.

It is possible to play the following pages of this book with either Double-Stroke or Multiple-Bounce Rolls, including the Sousa march charts. The exceptions are the John S. Pratt rudimental solos near the end of the book, in which all rolls should be played with the Double-Stroke technique.

Preparatory Exercises: the 5-Stroke Roll

LESSON 30
THE 5-STROKE ROLL

The 5-Stroke Roll is the shortest of the measured roll rudiments. It is played with three hand movements: two Double Strokes and a single, ending stroke to produce five strokes.

In examples a, b, and c below, you will need to apply the Double Stroke. Example c is shown three different ways, but all are played the same. Play slowly at first and work on the rebound with the wrist and fingers. Much written snare drum music will use ties with slashes across the stems. Some music will show only the slashes with no tie. You must count at all times and become familiar with the rhythmic abbreviations notated at the end of this book.

5-Stroke Roll Starting on the Downbeat

5-Stroke Roll Starting on the Upbeat

Now apply the Multiple-Bounce (concert) Roll. Begin with the same number of hand movements, but play Multiple-Bounce strokes instead of Double Strokes. When playing the Multiple-Bounce (concert) Roll at slower tempos, the number of hand movements may increase.

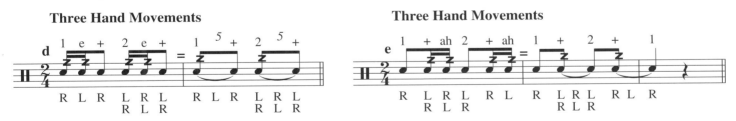

5-Stroke Roll Study

Practice tips: Practice with each approach to rolling. Sometimes accents appear at the beginning or end of a roll. Practice putting stress on these marked notes.

LESSON 31
5-STROKE ROLL EXERCISES

Practice tips: Count at all times. Practice with Double-Stroke and Multiple-Bounce Rolls. Apply alternate sticking with the Double-Stroke Roll and natural sticking with Multiple-Bounce rolls.

MR. HARR'S MARCH

In memory of Haskell Harr, percussion educator, performer, and author.
Former Head of Percussion at VanderCook College, Chicago, Illinois

Practice tips: This is a Traditional march chart in 2/4 featuring the 5-Stroke Roll. Note that the C section is marked as "Trio." The Trio is the third melody of a Traditional march composition. Tap your foot on the quarter-note pulse or play with a bass drummer.

LESSON 32
THE 9-STROKE ROLL

The 9-Stroke Roll is played with five hand movements: four Double Strokes and a single, ending stroke to produce nine strokes. The 9-Stroke Roll begins and ends with the same hand.

In examples a, b, and c below, apply the double-stroke technique. Example c is shown three different ways, but all are played the same. Play slowly at first and work on the rebound with the wrist and fingers. Count at all times.

9-Stroke Roll Starting on the Downbeat

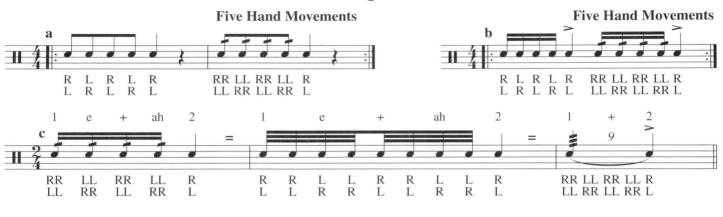

9-Stroke Roll Starting on the Upbeat

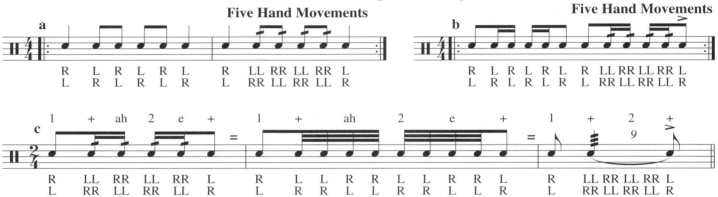

Now apply the Multiple-Bounce (concert) Roll. Begin with the same number of hand movements, but play Multiple-Bounce strokes instead of Double Strokes. When playing the Multiple-Bounce (concert) Roll at slower tempos, the number of hand movements may increase.

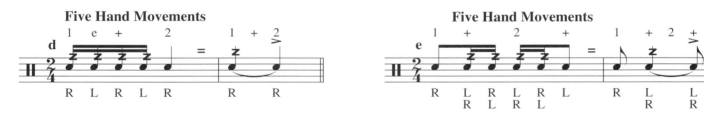

9-Stroke Roll Study

Practice tips: Work through the exercises in Lesson 33 to assist you in this study.

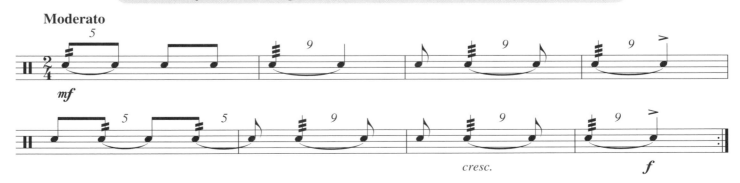

LESSON 33
9-STROKE ROLL EXERCISES

Practice tips: Practice all of these examples with Double-Stroke Open rolls and with Multiple-Bounce (concert-style) Rolls. Count all rhythms. Use left-hand lead also.

LESSON 34
5-STROKE AND 9-STROKE ROLL STUDIES

Practice tips: Practice with Double-Stroke (open) and Multiple-Bounce (concert-style) Rolls. Practice these studies at different tempos with *mp*, *mf*, and *f* dynamics. In addition, write in your own accents, crescendos, dynamic changes, and stickings.

Study I

Study II

Study III

Study IV

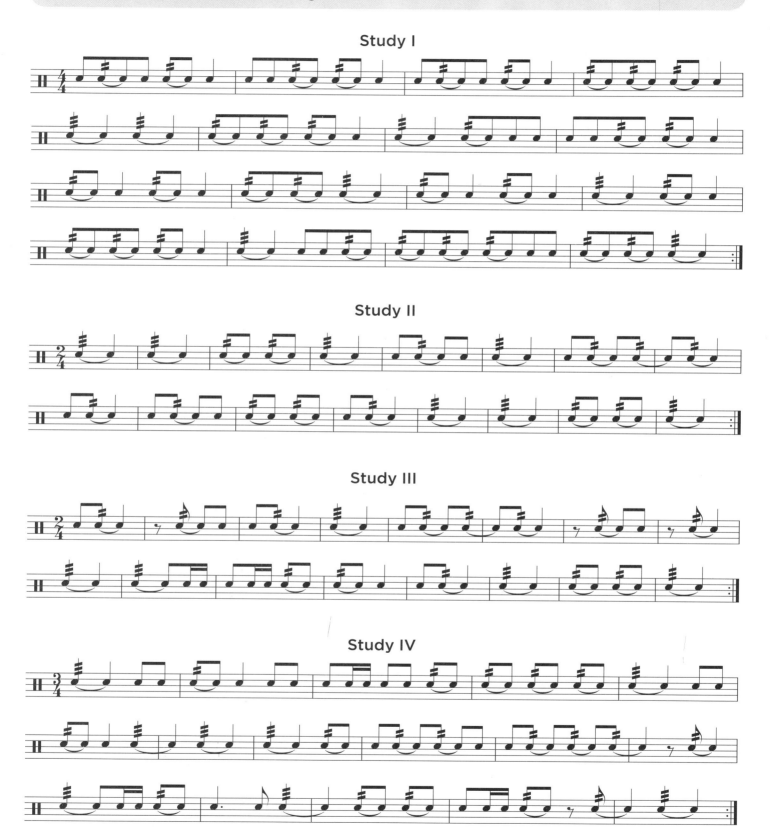

MR. SEWREY'S MARCH

Dedicated to Jim Sewrey, educator, conductor, performer, and author.
Named the Percussive Arts Society.
Percussion Instructor at Wisconsin Lutheran College, Milwaukee, Wisconsin

Practice tips: This Traditional march chart in 2/4 features 5-Stroke and 9-Stroke Rolls. Tap your foot on the quarter-note pulse or play with a bass drummer.

LESSON 35
13-STROKE, 15-STROKE, AND 17-STROKE ROLLS

Practice tips: Be sure to count when executing these longer rolls. Practice the following examples with Double-Stroke (open) Rolls and Multiple-Bounce (concert-style) Rolls. The 13-Stroke Roll gets its name from six Double Strokes and a single, ending stroke, made with seven hand movements. It begins and ends with the same hand. Practice with left-hand lead also. Work on finger and wrist action to play in both styles. When playing the Multiple-Bounce Roll, tempo will determine the number of hand movements.

13-Stroke Roll on the Downbeat

Concert-Style 13-Stroke Roll on the Downbeat

13-Stroke Roll on the Upbeat

Concert-Style 13-Stroke Roll on the Upbeat

Practice tips: The 15-Stroke Roll gets its name from seven Double Strokes and a single, ending stroke, played with eight hand movements. This roll ends on the opposite hand from which it starts. Practice starting with either hand.

15-Stroke Roll on the Downbeat

Concert-Style 15-Stroke Roll on the Downbeat

15-Stroke Roll on the "e" Beat

Concert-Style 15-Stroke Roll on the "e" Beat

Practice tips: The 17-Stroke Roll gets its name from eight Double Strokes and a single, ending stroke, made with nine hand movements. It begins and ends with the same hand. Practice with left-hand lead also.

17-Stroke Roll

Concert-Style 17-Stroke Roll

Practice tips: Although the 17-Stroke Roll is the longest numbered roll in rudimental drumming, longer rolls are sometimes notated by composers with the number of double strokes and a final note. See John S. Pratt's solo "Rubber Baby Buggy Bumpers" on page 67 for an example of this.

Concert-style rolls do not typically show the number of strokes above the roll, as they are made up of multiple, unmeasured bounces. When the number is shown, the player will generally play the roll with Double Strokes. The style of music and the type of drum called for in the music will also give the player a good idea as to how to interpret the roll notation.

Choose your sticking and roll style for the studies below.

Roll Study I

Roll Study II

MR. ROTHMAN'S MARCH

Dedicated to Joel Rothman of London, England, percussion educator and author

Practice tips: This Traditional march chart uses the 13-Stroke Roll. Be sure to count for correct rhythmic articulation.

MR. PORCARO'S MARCH

Dedicated to Joe Porcaro, percussionist, recording artist, author, and educator at Los Angeles Music Academy

Practice tips: This Traditional march chart features 15-Stroke and 17-Stroke Rolls. Be sure to count for correct rhythmic articulation.

LESSON 36

THE FLAM ♩

The Flam is a drum rudiment that consists of a grace note and a main note. The word "Flam" is onomatopoeia for the rudiment. Say "flaamm." It is one word with a slight stress at the beginning and end. The rudiment should sound like the word. The Flam's purpose is to extend the sound of the main note with the ornament of a single grace note. The grace note is indicated by a small ornament notated before the main note. It is not counted as a separate beat, and is played softly, slightly before the main note.

Right Flam

The right Flam consists of a left-hand grace note and a right-hand main note.

Left Flam

The left Flam consists of a right-hand grace note and a left-hand main note.

Alternating Flams

To play Traditional, alternating Flams, play the grace note as an upstroke and the main note as a downstroke.

Same Hand Flams

Another way to approach the Flam is to play the grace note as a tap and the main note as a full stroke, using the same hand positions.

A third approach is to play the grace note as a tap and the main note as a downstroke, using same-hand lead.

Although the Flam's grace note should be played very close to the main note, its sound can vary slightly depending on the genre of music being played. Rudimentally, the Flam is played slightly  "open"; in concert style, it is "closed." Be careful to not play the grace note and main note at the same time, as this will cancel out the drumhead's vibration and result in a "popping" sound. Generally called a "flat flam," this sound is called for in some modern drum charts, but is not the correct way to play the Traditional Flam rudiment. Another variation of the flat flam is the "double stop," where both sticks play from the same stick height simultaneously. Take great efforts to practice this rudiment so that it is executed correctly.

Flam Study

RUBBER BABY BUGGY BUMPERS

Dedicated to my six granddaughters: Kaitlin, Julia, Molly, Amanda, Kelsey, and Christmas

John S. Pratt, December 4, 2000

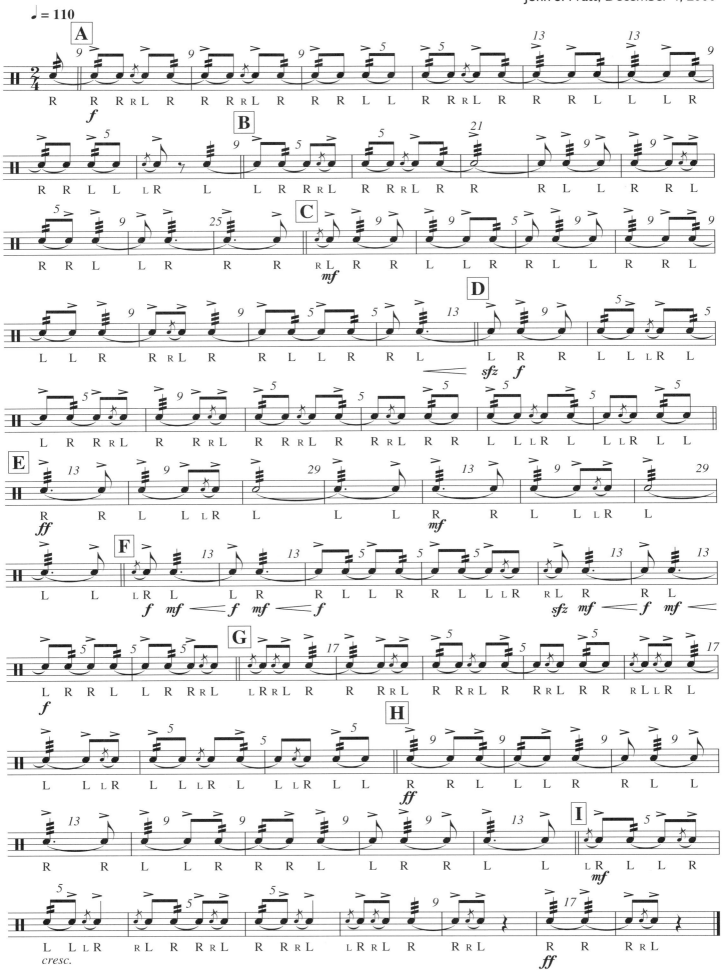

LESSON 37
THE DRAG  AND RUFFS

The Drag is a drum rudiment that consists of two ornamental grace notes and a main note. The word "Drag" is used by many modern percussionists for this rudiment, but some refer to this rudiment by its Traditional name, the Ruff. Like the Flam, the Drag is designated right or left by its main note.

Articulation: In the open, Traditional rudimental approach, the grace notes are clean and heard as two distinct grace notes leading into the main note. In the closed, concert-style approach, the grace notes are closer to the main note and often interpreted as a buzz sound leading into the main note.

The grace notes are played softer than the main note. Much practice is needed to be able to articulate this rudiment. Be aware of the style of music you are playing. As with the Flam, the Drag can be attached to any main note value, and the ornamental notes are not counted.

The Drag

The Alternating 3-Stroke Ruff

The alternating 3-Stroke Ruff consists of two alternating grace notes and a main note. Besides its application to snare drumming, it is of great use to percussionists when playing other percussion instruments and is important to master.

The 4-Stroke Ruff

The alternating 4-Stroke Ruff (also called the single-stroke 4 when counted and played on the beat in rudimental drumming) consists of four alternating notes. The 4-Stroke Ruff contains three ornamental grace notes and a final main note. In the example below, the grace notes should be played softer than the main note. Some great examples of sticking variations for the rudiment can be found in George Lawrence Stone's book *Accents and Rebounds* on page 21. Stone's book is an excellent technique study and is recommended by the authors.

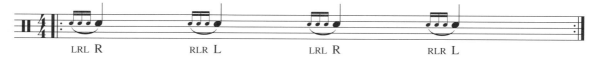

In the same fashion as above, more alternating grace notes can be added to the main note to create the 5-stroke ruff, 6-stroke ruff, and so on. Examples of longer single-stroke ruffs can be found in much snare drum literature.

Study Featuring Ornamental Grace Notes

LESSON 38
THE TWO FEEL

¢ or $\frac{2}{2}$ Counts in measure
Half note receives the beat (count)

Cut-Time

Often, in martial music, you will need to count "in two." Simply stated, because you march with two feet, some music will be played in a feeling of two—especially marches. Our first example of this feel is cut-time, which is felt in two and is indicated by a time signature of a ¢ with a slash through it ¢. It is also seen written with a 2/2 time signature. In either case, you count two half-note beat pulses in each measure and feel all the rhythms in double time. While counting in two (although it looks like 4/4), the quarter note will feel like an eighth note, the eighth note will feel like a sixteenth note, and so on.

When playing rolls in cut-time, you will also double the counting. The quarter note will feel like an eighth, the eighth note will feel like a sixteenth, and so on. Apply the roll to the eighth-note pulse.

6/8 "In Two"

To feel martial music in a quick 6/8 march, you will also need to count "in two." Feel the triple rhythms in a duple (double) feel, where the dotted-quarter receives the beat. When playing the roll, bounce on the eighth-note pulse. Play the examples below and apply them to the Sousa marches on the next page. Rolls can be interpreted as double-stroke or multiple-stroke.

EL CAPITAN AND THE WASHINGTON POST

Practice tips: Some band and orchestra parts use a single line to notate the snare drum part. Practice these parts and obtain recordings of these famous marches so you can play along to the melodies of the legendary American composer and bandleader John Phillip Sousa.

El Capitan

John Phillip Sousa

The Washington Post

John Phillip Sousa

LESSON 39
THE 7-STROKE ROLL

The 7-Stroke Roll is played with four hand movements: three Double Strokes and a single, ending stroke, producing seven strokes. It ends on the opposite hand from which it starts. The 7-Stroke Roll is used Traditionally to lead into music as a "pick-up" beat. It can also be started on the downbeat.

In examples a, b, and c, you need to apply Double-Stroke technique. Example c is shown three different ways, but all are played the same. Play slowly at first and work on the rebound with the wrist and fingers. Count at all times.

7-Stroke Roll Starting on the Downbeat

7-Stroke Roll Starting on the "e" Beat

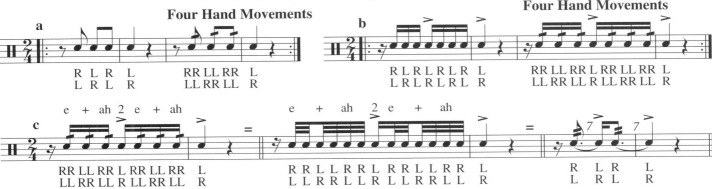

7-Stroke Roll Starting on the Downbeat and the "and" Beat

The 7-Stroke Roll is felt as a triplet in Traditional rudimental drumming. Practice this rhythmic variation as well. When used as a "pick-up" in Traditional drumming it is most often started with the left hand.

7-Stroke Roll Starting on the Downbeat

7-Stroke Roll Starting on the Upbeat

Practice tips: Practice the Multiple-Bounce (concert) Roll in all of the rhythmic feels above. 7-Stroke Rolls can be substituted for 5-Stroke Rolls in some situations.

Study Using the 7-Stroke Roll

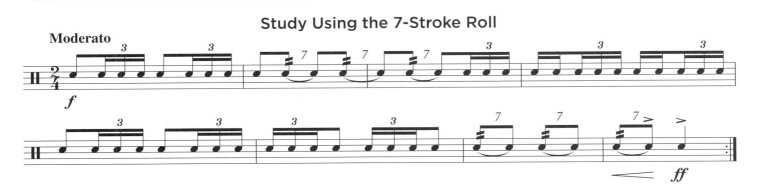

THERE'S A SCREW LOOSE SOMEWHERE

John S. Pratt

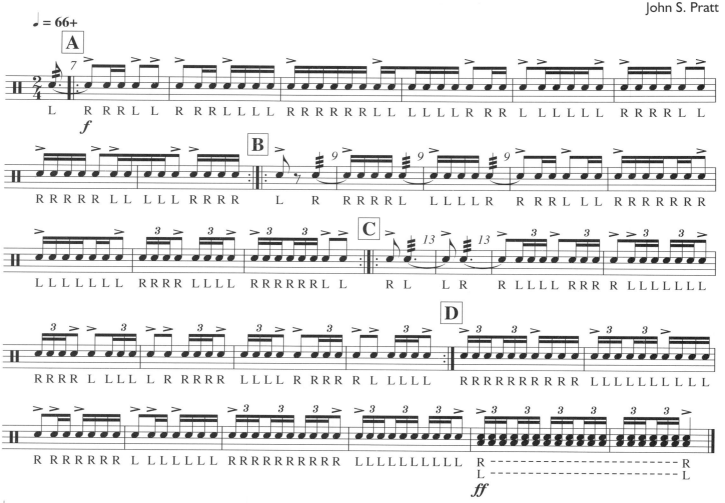

♩ = Double stop: play both sticks at the same time from the same height.

LESSON 40
DRUM RUDIMENTS

Practice tips: In the following rudimental drum solos by John S. Pratt, look for these drum rudiments. Practice each rudiment on its own, and then apply them musically in the solos. In addition, practice each in Traditional rudimental style, where each one is played slow to fast to slow.

For more information regarding the rudiments, refer to the book *The 26 Traditional American Drumming Rudiments* by John S. Pratt.

Single Paradiddle
The Single Paradiddle is a combination of two alternating strokes followed by a double stroke.

Double Paradiddle
The Double Paradiddle is a combination of four alternating strokes followed by a double stroke.

Triple Paradiddle

The Triple Paradiddle is a combination of six alternating strokes followed by a double stroke.

R L R L R L R R   L R L R L R L L

Paradiddle-Diddle

The Paradiddle-Diddle consists of a Single Paradiddle followed by another double stroke. It is often played as a sextuplet.

R L R R L L R L R R L L R L R R L L R L R R L L
L R L L R R L R L L R R L R L L R R L R L L R R

Single-Stroke Seven

The Single-Stroke Seven is played as seven single strokes. It is often played as a sextuplet.

R L R L R L R   L R L R L R L   R L R L R L R   L R L R L R L

Flam Paradiddle

The Flam Paradiddle is a Single Paradiddle preceded by a grace note.

l R L R R rL R L L   l R L R R rL R L L

Flam Paradiddle-Diddle

The Flam Paradiddle-Diddle is a Paradiddle-Diddle preceded by a grace note.

l R L R R L L lrL R L L R R   l R L R R L L lrL R L L R R

Flamacue

The Flamacue is a Flam followed by three single notes and a final Flam. The second note is accented. It is the only truly American rudiment (not of European origin) of the 26 Standard Rudiments. It is Traditionally played as starting with a right-hand Flam, but became used more often with a left-hand lead as developed in solos by John S. Pratt in the mid-20th century.

l R   L   R   L l R   l R   L   R   L l R
r L   R   L   R r L   r L   R   L   R r L

Flam Accent

The Flam Accent is a Flam followed by two alternating strokes. It is often written as a triplet, but can also be phrased as sixteenth notes.

l R L R rL R L   l R L R rL R L lL R L   R rL R L lL R L
r L R L lL R L   r L R L lL R L rL R L lL R L rL R L

Flam Tap

The Flam Tap consists of a Flam followed by a single note played with the same hand as the main note of the Flam.

l R   R   rL   L   l R   R   rL   L   l R   R   rL   L

REINDEERS ON THE ROOFTOP
AND SANTA CLAUS WITH A BAG OF TOYS FOR MY
GRANDDAUGHTER, CHRISTMAS HOLLY TRINITY

John S. Pratt, December 25, 2010

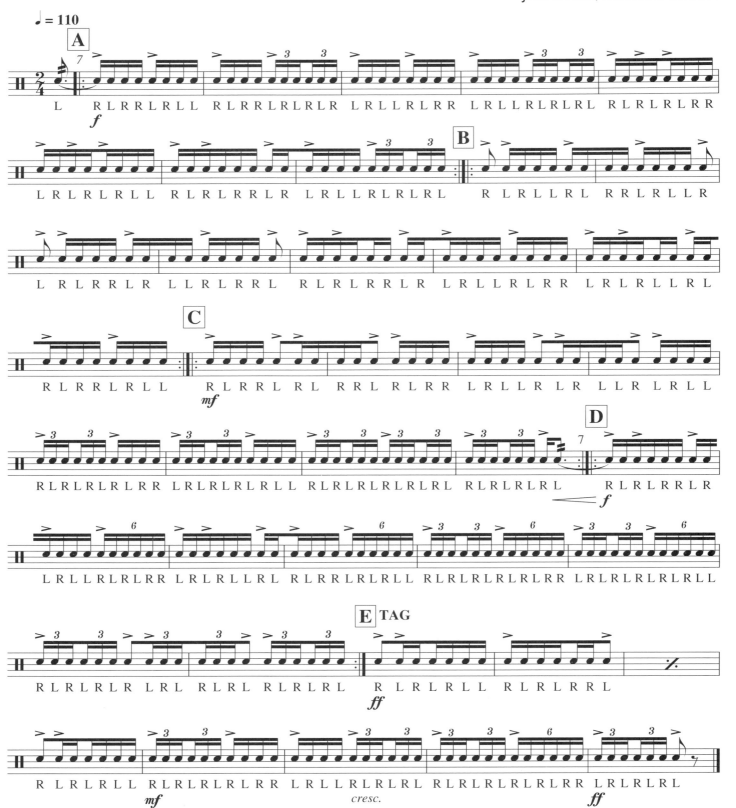

DOUBLE PARADIDDLE THUMPSTER

Dedicated to Jeff Salisbury, percussion instructor, the University of Vermont

John S. Pratt

JUST FEELING THE FLAMACUE
AND 7/13/19-STROKE SINGLETS

Dedicated to my grandson, Kyle Fitzsimons

John S. Pratt

* This solo fits the melody of "Waltzing Matilda" or "U.S. Marine's Hymn."

HI BOOTS!

John S. Pratt, 2003

GRANDSON STERLING, KEEP BANGING AWAY ON YOUR DRUM!

John S. Pratt, 2011

* Inverted Flam Tap

** The 5-Stroke Roll is to be played as a grace note and should be played as a "squeezed" 5-Stroke Roll that must be fit into the note rhythm. For additional study using this technique, see *Rudimental Solos for Accomplished Drummers* by John S. Pratt, published by Meredith Music.

RHYTHMIC ABBREVIATIONS
Common Examples of Rhythmic Abbreviations

ABBREVIATIONS WITH EIGHTH NOTES

ABBREVIATIONS WITH SIXTEENTH NOTES

ABBREVIATIONS WITH THIRTY-SECOND NOTES

ABBREVIATIONS WITH DOTTED NOTES

tr〜〜〜 The trill (or tremolo) marked above a note signifies that a roll should be played. Play the roll for the duration of the notes marked. The tr〜〜〜 marking can sometimes appear along with ties to additional notes.

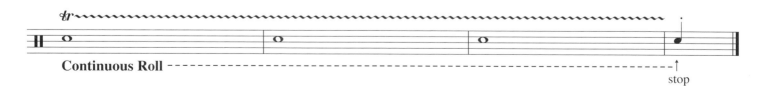

Continuous Roll - ↑
stop

FOCUS ON FUNDAMENTALS
WITH HAL LEONARD SNARE DRUM BOOKS

HAL LEONARD SNARE DRUM METHOD
The Musical Approach to Snare Drum for Band and Orchestra
by Rick Mattingly

Geared toward beginning band and orchestra students, this modern, musical approach to learning snare drum includes a play-along CD that features full concert band recordings of band arrangements and classic marches with complete drum parts that allow the beginning drummer to apply the book's lessons in a realistic way. This book/CD pack also includes: fun-to-play solos and etudes; duets that can be played with another drummer, a teacher, or with the play-along tracks on the CD; studies in 4/4, 2/4, 3/4, 6/8 and cut-time; roll studies; and much more!
06620059 Book/CD Pack
.... $10.99

40 INTERMEDIATE SNARE DRUM SOLOS
by Ben Hans

This book is designed as a lesson supplement, or as performance material for recitals and solo competitions. Includes: 40 intermediate snare drum solos presented in easy-to-read notation; a music glossary; Percussive Arts Society rudiment chart; suggested sticking, dynamics and articulation markings; and much more!
06620067 .... $7.95

INNER RHYTHMS – MODERN STUDIES FOR SNARE DRUM
by Frank Colonnato

This intermediate to advanced-level book presents interesting and challenging etudes for snare drum based on the rhythms of contemporary music, including a variety of time signatures, shifting meters and a full range of dynamics. These studies will help improve reading skills as well as snare drum technique.
06620017 .... $7.95

SNARE DRUM PLAY-ALONG
by Joe Cox

This book has been designed to help intermediate and advanced drummers develop rudiment speed with play-along tracks that start slowly, accelerate, then slow back down. But what sets it apart from other rudiment books is musical grooves, in a number of different styles, which help the drummer to hear the sticking patterns. The melodies in the tracks mirror and/or compliment the left and right hands of the rudiment.
06620141 Book/CD Pack
.... $14.99

RUDIMENTAL DRUM SOLOS FOR THE MARCHING SNARE DRUMMER
by Ben Hans

Meant as a study for developing the rudiments in a musical manner, this book is designed as a progressive lesson supplement and as performance material for recitals, contests, and solo competitions. Includes: solos featuring N.A.R.D., P.A.S., and hybrid drum rudiments; warm-up exercises; and more.
06620074 .... $12.95

Prices, contents and availability subject to change without notice.

SNARE DRUM SOLOS
Seven Pieces for Concert Performance
by Sperie Karas

These solos provide excellent performance material for recitals and solo competition, and are perfect for use as lesson supplements. Seven solos include: The Fast Track • Hot News • Lay It Down • The Right Touch • Rollin' and Rockin' • Strollin' on Six • Waltz for Jazzers.
06620079 .... $5.95

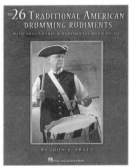

THE 26 TRADITIONAL AMERICAN DRUMMING RUDIMENTS
by John S. Pratt

This collection of rudimental examples and roll charts will aid the learner in mastering the rudimental language. John S. Pratt's early works, now once again available, are an essential part of America's "traditional" drumming heritage. This new edition contains a new foreword and corrected music engravings, and also includes the classic solos "The Sons of Liberty" and "The All-American Emblem."
06620124 .... $9.99

128 RUDIMENTAL STREET BEATS, ROLLOFFS, AND PARADE-SONG PARTS
by John S. Pratt

This book contains "traditional" rudimental selections for snare, tenor, and bass drums that will provide the drum sections of parade or drilling units a varied repertoire of performance material. Contains a CD of the material performed by the author, helpful exercises for intermediate drummers, and a preface and foreword.
06620123 Book/CD Pack
.... $14.99

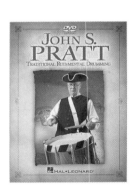

TRADITIONAL RUDIMENTAL DRUMMING *DVD*
by John S. Pratt

In this DVD, John S. Pratt will reinvigorate your study of "traditional" ancient rudimental drumming and provide material for your practice, instruction, music library and drumming pleasure. The DVD includes: classic and new Pratt solos • four original Pratt compositions in the "Spirit of 1776" rope tension snare and bass drum duets with Ben Hans • printable scores on disc • and more.
00320825 DVD-ROM .. $24.99

FOR MORE INFORMATION, SEE YOUR LOCAL MUSIC DEALER, OR WRITE TO:

HAL•LEONARD®
CORPORATION
7777 W. BLUEMOUND RD. P.O. BOX 13819
MILWAUKEE, WISCONSIN 53213

www.halleonard.com

0812